RAINBOW WARRIOR

poems by

Jacquelyn Markham

Finishing Line Press
Georgetown, Kentucky

RAINBOW WARRIOR

ACKNOWLEDGMENTS

"A Child Speaks to Libokra," *Peering Into the Iris: An Ancestral Journey*,
Jacquelyn Markham, 2008. *Hawai'i Pacific Review*, Hawai'i Pacific University,
HI, December, 2016
"The Day Snow Fell Close to the Equator," *Poets for A Livable Planet*, Los
Angeles, Vol. I, July, 1991. Finalist, Rita Dove Poetry Award, Salem College
International Literary Awards, Salem, NC, 2012 (with title "It Seemed A
Miracle of Snow")
"Myth of the Infinite Sea," *Anthology of Appalachian Writers*, Shepherd
University, WV, Vol. IV, March, 2012
"Full Moon," *Magical Blend: A Transformative Journey*, San Francisco, CA.
1986. *Peering Into the Iris: An Ancestral Journey*, Jacquelyn Markham, 2008

Publisher: Leah Huete de Maines
Editor: Christen Kincaid
Cover Art: *Mother of the Sea* by Jacquelyn Markham
Interior Photos: Courtesy of Greenpeace
Author Photo: Mary Jett
Cover Design: Elizabeth Maines McCleavy

Order online: www.finishinglinepress.com
also available on amazon.com

Author inquiries and mail orders:
Finishing Line Press
PO Box 1626
Georgetown, Kentucky 40324
USA

Table of Contents

Dedicated to Rachel Carson

a Bikinian lament

Even in dreams I cannot be happy
Dreams of my homeland bring sorrow
I sleep on my mat and pillow
dream of the atoll I love
dream of the atoll I know
I hear the sounds of waves kissing the blue lagoon
of my dreams

Dreams of my homeland bring memories
Memories of my homeland bring sorrow

I wake with the pain and I weep
because even in dreams I cannot be happy
Nothing can be right for me

Adapted from a Bikinian song, translated by P. Drucker

BIKINI ATOLL

aqua blue sun-swimming waves
clear living waves
slippery glass waves slide
mirror blue pile up
slide up on shore white shore
cradles blue to the horizon
blue over blue centuries of blue
palms sway in salt air
swish of palms with the dawn
swish of palms with the night
azure blue with the dawn
indigo blue with the night

children glide like brown fish
in shallows at sunrise
Juda sails the sunlit lagoon
Meija weaves in a fish
on the basket of palm fronds
and she weaves in the sun
she weaves fish and the sun
sets on canoes sailing home

children stop play in the waves
mothers pack babies in baskets like bundles
fathers carry sons & sons carry fathers
grandfathers bring fish swimming silver in memory
grandmothers remember canoes in red sunsets
        remember canoes sailing home

ships transport people away

oblivious blue slides over reef
oblivious wind skims over surf
wind skims shore

wind bends trees
wind lifts wings
planes fly to Bikini Atoll
men turn themselves into gods

II.

Bombs explode on Bikini Atoll
one hundred times the power of Hiroshima
one thousand times the power of Hiroshima

the sand
the shells
the fish
the crab
the turtle
the blue blue liquid rolling in
the arrowroot
the coconut
the milk
the pandanus tree
the worm
the bird
the dreams
the graves
the lives of Bikini Atoll

Vanish

This is only a test
This is only a test

If an actual emergency occurs...

I repeat

This is only a test

A CHILD SPEAKS TO LIBOKRA

*The elders claim that Libokra, an evil female spirit, once lived
in the southern Marshalls where Rongerik was originally located.
She stole the atoll, hid it among the northern islands, &
attempted to settle at Bikini. Libokra was driven off by Orijabato,
a benevolent male spirit who resided there & guarded the
Bikinians. Libokra fled and everywhere she visited, the story
goes, fish were poisoned & crops declined. At last, her body, cast
into the lagoon, poisoned the fish that since then make people
sick when eaten.*

Libokra, my father said it was you
that came to Bikini before the people had to leave
and that Orijabato drove you off
because you were evil

Libokra, the chief said it was you that came and stole away
Rongerik in the night and moved the island
from south to north and then the fish began to make us sick
and the palm trees died and the sandy isle
became sandier so nothing would grow

Libokra, they said they killed you
and dropped your bones in the sea
and the fish who nibbled there
became poison to us and we could not eat
Libokra, they said it was you but I know it isn't true

Remember the night before the big ships came to Bikini
I sneaked away from the hut
rising quietly from my mat to say goodbye to the lagoon
I walked alone under the full moon
the waves seemed lonelier than ever before
the palms gave mournful sounds
and though I often went to the graves at night
where my sister was buried

and though the moon scattered light over the shore
and the water glistened as in sunlight
I felt afraid and a chill blew through my shift
and even the ones buried seemed to weep at the mournful
sound of the palms

Libokra, then I saw you rise up from the sea
above me, bigger than my mother
or even Mejia, the strongest woman on Bikini
your long black hair covered with seaweed
your body bare and swimming like a fish

you dipped and splashed
not playful like a porpoise
but like you were angry and swimming desperately your last time
as I do when mother calls me to come in at sunset
and I don't want to come ashore

I watched you dive down and scoop up a great shell
I couldn't move but I wasn't afraid anymore
I felt safe and protected like my mother was near
and you began to speak to me
"Listen to the shell
the whisper of the sea—never forget
no matter how they try to destroy me, I will return"

you offered me a spiraling shell
saying "tell all who hear the spirit of the sea
they will drive me away
they will kill me
they will defile my name
but my mother is the sea
the unending and eternal sea"

I touched your skin which was warm
not cold like a fish
I smelled your saltiness
I wanted to ask "will they believe me?"
but you dove under and swiftly swam away

The moon until then bright and beaming down
spun around turning dark and darker
plunged into the water
lost like a huge rock into the waves
I stood on the shore like a rock myself
until I heard my mother call

Looking up, I saw the moon was there as always
palms dancing like every night before
sand damp and warm under my feet
in my hand the shell Libokra gave me
I put the shell to my ear and my mother's voice
faded into the night
I heard at first Libokra saying
tell all who hear the spirit of the sea
then only a whispering:

I am the mother of the sea
I am the mother of the sea

RAINBOW WARRIOR

for the people of Rongelap leaving home on the Rainbow Warrior
escaping radioactive fallout from nuclear testing**

Rainbow Warrior cradles the ones from Rongelap
tossed in the night's black sea
lulling sea   a lullaby in night's indigo sky
moon's bright beam washes white
the bow that plunges low
reaches high to glittery stars
mast punctures dark seal of sky
releases bits of salted air
to taste on tips of tongues
wind weaving wisps of hair
a magic web of sleep draping shoulders
like nets of fallen stars

Rainbow Warrior cradles the ones from Rongelap
until a rainbow arcs the morning sky—breaks
a million tiny colored beads
bounce on ocean blue
splash on lashes of Meja and Mejo
children waking now with sunlit tears
wondering where are our beds?
wondering where this big ship goes?
and never looking back to Rongelap
mothers   fathers   elders   children
wondering why this morning
it is raining tears and rainbows

Rainbow Warrior. 1. There is a popular myth, attributed to the Cree
Indian nation, that a Rainbow Warrior will descend from the sky to save
those on earth from extinction. 2. The Rainbow Warrior, a Greenpeace
ship that relocated the people of Rongelap from their contaminated island
in the south Pacific.

THE DAY SNOW FELL CLOSE TO THE EQUATOR

for all the people of Rongelap*

Ash and coral burst into the sky
swirled east of Bikini
frolicked in the winds
fell to a child's wonder in silence
on Rongelap below
bits of ash and coral
coral from the morning sky seemed a miracle of snow
and like a rare snowstorm in the South
beckoned them to play
to taste the powder on the sand

but unlike snow it wasn't cool to skin
but as Iroji Kebenli found
it burned the skin right off
and as Lekoj Anjain found
to taste it made you very sick
and as Lekoj's family found
it killed a young man as quickly as an old

Nearby the fisherman of Lucky Dragon No.5
their awe short-lived
not strangers to the bomb
of Nagasaki—Hiroshima
they prayed all night long for the fisherman who died
as if they sensed the omen
the day it seemed a miracle of snow
fell close to the equator

**one day in 1954 Bravo, a 15 megaton hydrogen bomb detonated on
Bikini Atoll in the South Pacific. Radioactive ash and coral drifted east
over the island of Rongelap.*

TWO WORLDS

for the women of the lush and tropical Pacific Islands who suffer
from radiation from testing of atomic and hydrogen bombs,
exploded on land, in air, underwater, and on barges in their
homelands for many years

I.

I live in two separate worlds: one part of me wants to have a baby,
but this other part of me is too scared.
Lijon Eknilang (1946-2012), Rongelap Atoll

I live in two worlds
in one I want to have a child
in another I am afraid
in one I feel happiness
in another I feel fear

after nine months of growing round and drum tight
the labor table presses cold against my back
pain pushes through my belly
like machetes slash coconuts in two
with one swift movement
milk pours out
warm and white the sand soaks up the liquid
waves in slow rhythm wash the blue lagoon
where warm and clear the water slides over and under me
waves wash over me
whirlpools swirl in eddies
kiss me while I float back
squint rainbows from the sun
fish nibble my toes
schools of silver fish glimmer by
mother scolds because I splash them away
scatter them from silver nets
I don't care and laugh
I splash and waves wash over me

II

Now we have this problem of what we call jelly-fish babies. These babies are born like jelly-fish. This ugly "thing" only lives for a few hours. When they die they are buried right away.
Darlene Keju-Johnson (1951-1996), Ebeye Island

We live in two worlds
the ocean is our supermarket
the ocean is our spirit

We live in two worlds
the ocean teems with fish
glowing radioactive
contaminated
the ocean is killing us slowly

We live in two worlds
here—babies are born like jelly-fish
there—the spirit of the water whispers to me
she beckons me to save her
and I plunge into the water trying
yet I wonder *will we survive?*
or will she suck me under?

Her dark blue waters
womb or grave?

MYTH OF THE INFINITE SEA

"...the sea, though changed in a sinister way, will continue to exist; the threat is rather to life itself." Rachel Carson, The Sea Around Us

1

The Carolina Chickadee arrives for the seed,
the Cardinal Scarlets into sight,
the Pileated Woodpecker just beyond pounds the pine,
Blue Jays dive into the Japanese tub I made them
while their downy offspring hop the garden rows.
Mockingbird and Brown Thrasher have come to peace.
Doves coo and peck and fly with flourish of wing-beat.
Oh, a Bluebird song in the distance! And look there! A Yellow Bird!
Out front a Hummingbird sucks the red bottlebrush blooms,
the Canadian Geese honk low overhead,
Egrets dance with swooping grace.
A white sky island morning along the Gulf Stream.

2

*"I sense my limit
my shell-jaws snap shut at invasion of the limitless,
ocean-weight: infinite water. . ." H.D.*

I see the headline an early April morning:
my shell-jaws snap shut

Bit by bit into my consciousness: explosion, oil spill,
oil release, rig, oil globules, top kill, orange foam.

Bit by bit into my consciousness: oil spews,
chemical dispersants, crude oil, barrels,
oiled birds, burning black billows of smoke,
oil sheen, oil plumes beneath the waves.

Bit by bit, I let it in—an invasion of the limitless.
I sense my limit.

3

"there has long been a certain comfort in the belief
that the sea, at least was inviolate,
But this belief, unfortunately, has proved to be naïve..."
Rachel Carson

"Infinite water" is not infinite water

We thought the sea *inviolate*
We thought the sea *limitless*
We used the sea as atomic wasteland
oil and water: infinite sea is not infinite.

4

Oyster Catchers, Herons, Ibis,
Pelicans, Osprey, Terns, the precious Marsh Sparrow.
It is Spring! Mating! Nesting!
Sea Turtles, Porpoise, shining Yellow Fin Tuna.
Pas a Loutre, Chandeleur Islands, millions of gallons a day,
oil slides in with night tide.
Mississippi Delta, fresh water marshes, rookeries,
oiled birds, Brown Pelicans, delicate plumaged Egrets.
Cleanse the river of my soul.

5

I imagine myself an Eagle
above the confluence—
Ashepoo, Combahee, Edisto Rivers
where my nest sits high in a pine,
tide rises over the sandbar where a pair of
orange-eyed Oyster Catchers nest and sun.

I imagine traveling high above the creek,
island after island to the mouth of the big river,
narrowing to what I know as Lucy Creek.
I am an Eagle and know no names
only water and land—the wide and mutable
river meandering salty marshes.
I leave Beaufort behind,
crossing the Albergotti Creek to north and cross again
black waters of Combahee, Ashepoo, Edisto
through lowlands of Green Pond and great swamp sanctuary
Water Lilies, Alligators, Heron,
up a light incline to dry land and cotton fields for a time,
toward Columbia, Saluda River
still beyond, another twenty miles, by foot
a day's walk toward the mountain streams.

I imagine this distance I have journeyed
slimed with oil, pumped from the earth's
center—out of place,
penetrating, saturating, smothering, poisoning.
This distance is the vastness of the oil
still pumping, pouring, poisoning sea to shore.

This journey I make as Eagle
to comprehend the vastness—not of the sea, but of the oil on the sea
amoeba-like, it shifts, patterns, abstractions,
"oil painted" images from air, from sea, from land,
disaster documented digitized infinite images
heavy, moderate, light, oil shape-shifting.
NOAA maps the trajectory as if a missile or a bullet,
not millions of gallons of crude oil
erupting like a volcano under the sea.
Shape-shifting, now the black, the brown, the red
a deep sea "oil plume" 15 miles across? More and changing,

3,300 feet deep? More and shifting, moving,
amoeba-like, separating, growing.
What do numbers matter? Numbers change as currents do
currency, how many dollars a day are lost?
How many made?

6

Numbers: Brown Pelican, 41 inches length
darker flight feathers on a 90-inch wingspan.
Brown Pelican plunges from great heights
to water to catch fish.
Brown Pelican, chestnut nape and neck,
yellow crown, white head, soft gray-brown body plumage,
fluttering to sea for fish.
May 23rd, 2010, a month after the rig's explosion at sea,
oil invades two Brown Pelican rookeries in Barataria Bay,
Gulf of Mexico.

7

Brown Pelican dives deep from great heights
Brown Pelican soaring skies on wind currents
dives deep, returns to rookery,
a colony of life, encircled by protective booms,
surrounded by oily death
gold crown of the Brown Pelican in sunlight gleams
with silvery fish an offering to nest-mate,
Brown Pelican from the skies
wingspan more than 7 feet of grace,
Brown Pelican struggles to escape "rescuers" nets
Brown Pelican saturated with crude oil
Brown Pelican weighted cannot fly
Calamity—*spill*
Catastrophe—*release*
Disaster.

"tiny organisms are eaten by larger ones and so on up the food chain…by such a process tuna over an area of a million square miles surrounding the Bikini bomb test developed a degree of radioactivity enormously higher than that of the sea water" Rachel Carson

Underwater, the Cousteaus' first dive
into the "nightmare,"
bring the moving images to us
oil particles infinite, limitless
snow in a blizzard.
Man-o-war oil tangled in dead sea,
disaster digitized on screens—
atomic mushrooms
My Lai
twin towers
oil gusher of Deepwater Horizon.
All attempts: cap, top kill, junk kill, robot
on live cam we watch—all futile.
May day, May day
Memorial Day, 2010
memorial to the life that we knew.

Passerina Ciris, Painted Bunting
pair at the feeder—look quickly!
Fluorescent red, green and purple he;
iridescent green she.
Brilliant plumage, yet hard to see
having learned the foolish will cage them.
A bird in the hand not worth two in the bush.
Infinite sea not infinite.

A white-skied July morning now,
Oil plumes in the Gulf billow black—
infinite sea not infinite,
a dream out of the mist.

THE LONG NIGHT MOON: RONDEAU

The long night moon and sea tides rise.
The long night moon's glorious size
  Floods the sea and vast savanna,
  Golden glow on the campagna.
Hypnotic, we follow coastwise.

Dancing moonbeams spill from the skies.
On Harbor River currents vaporize,
Creating a magical arcana
  To meet the long night moon!

Moonlight and river hypnotize
Us. Ocean pulls as tide rises.
  Beyond spartina and manna
  Grasses. Pursuing nirvana—
Perfect union—ocean rises
  To meet the long night moon!

Flicker Montage

1

A crescent breast. A patch of red.
What brings this pair of Flickers, strangers,
to my leaf strewn yard this winter afternoon?
An abstract painting laced with browns against a splash of red.
Tones of ocher, umber, sienna, sepia: squirrel, Sparrow,
Oak leaf, bark of trees. Flickers,
family of the Ivory Billed Woodpecker, landed
on this lowcountry island for rest,
clear water, grubs drilled from leaf clutter snug in the dirt.

2

A Montana trail, Summer Solstice, startled on my walk
by a flock of Bohemian Waxwings. Beavers roll and
play in dark, cold waters, pulling grasses along the
bank of river whirling brown. I spot a crescent breast,
a patch of red, Northern Flicker, ratatattat on the riverbank.

3

As a girl, I breathed deeply the minty scent,
wandered the fields and creek beds, brook babble
falling over stones. Highest tops of Poplars called my name—
wind whispered secrets in the Cottonwoods.
Rabbits nibbled overripe pears dropped to the ground,
tame enough to touch, wild brown fur
softer than the bank of grass.
Lilacs and Forsythia in spring and ice castles in winter, but always
scent of mint and sound of creek and pheasant rush.
I followed the water sound, like the raccoon, the mink, the deer.

4

Today a winter Bluebird splashes in the bath after
a cold snap while geese fly overhead trailing primal sounds.

5

Inside, my desktop screen, a montage of dark scenes:

Cyprus. A million songbirds trapped & slaughtered for
a chef's gourmet dish.

New Zealand. Blue Penguins oiled in a quiet spill, the *MV Rena*—
not Valdez, not BP Deepwater Horizon, not Texas coast vast
pollution—out of our radar, on a video, a small spill spoiling
Blue Penguins on Papamoa beach.

Durango, Mexico: The last Imperial Woodpecker, female, blur of
ghostly images, 16 mm camera handheld by Dr. Rhein on a mule
in 1956. Logging felled tree after tree, every home for the Imperial,
now extinct with the Ivory Billed.

6

Vernal Equinox. A week has passed since the Cedar Waxwing
lighted—alone and could not fly. I sit with it now as it breakfasts
on Holly berries. Azaleas bloom. Birdsong punctuates the morning
sunlight from every direction, except the mute and puzzled
Waxwing who cocks its head and listens. Days later, she hops up
to twigs in a bush, feeds on insects at dusk. Great Egrets fly toward
the pond as light fades. Another day, the Waxwing weaves her way
up high in the Live Oak. That night I dreamed she could fly.

7

Here, on this island, a rare sighting of Flickers that grace my world.
Crescent breast like new moon rising crimson,
brightens winter landscape. Flickers throw dirt like confetti,
call *wik wik wik klee yer!*

SITTA PUSILLA

A visitor with chestnut crown, Sitta Pusilla whistle sings
to me each time I step near the old lamp post,
the annual home and nest of this brown-headed nuthatch.
She tucks her nest into a crevice
where a gas light once flamed.
Male companions swoop in waves
as if to tie ribbons in the air for her.
And more, they have come to help with parenting.
Her tiny beak taps the metal, drills
the vintage post for minute specks of insects
that only she perceives. Perhaps a distraction from
the nesting duties and a way to stay nearby.
Fledglings, if they hatch, the size of pennies
glow copper in the sun, mimicking whistle songs
with mouths wide open. Then, one day silence strikes me
when I chance by and peek inside to the quiet nest.

FULL MOON

Round drum tight belly
embryonic tides ebb flow
the moon ripens
as the Navaho waits for its pull

In the rain forest
the moth orchid
accepts the random moth
if not broken by wind or rain
in its years' slow opening

And I
like the moth orchid
open my petals to the moon
tides swell in me
I wax
I wane
She gives birth
The orchid blooms
My child-self takes form
Ink flows like blood

Tides turn
moon sets
the horizon pushes
the sun out to the red sky

Jacquelyn Markham, author of two chapbooks and a personal mythology, *Peering Into the Iris: An Ancestral Journey*, has published nationally and internationally in literary journals, magazines, and anthologies, including *Archive: South Carolina Poetry Since 2005, Adrienne Rich: A Tribute Anthology, Anthology of Appalachian Writers, Lullwater Review, Hawaii Pacific Review, The High Window, Woman and Earth*, among others. Some of the poems in *Rainbow Warrior* are part of a larger collection emerging from her extensive research on nuclear testing conducted at the Marshall Islands during the 1940s and 50s. Others reflect her love of nature and earth centered spirituality.

During her academic career, Markham's love of poetry extended to scholarship as she "rescued" 19th century women poets who had fallen into obscurity. Focusing on collecting the far-flung poems by Charlotte Perkins Gilman, Markham published the award-winning reference *The Complete Poetry of Charlotte Perkins Gilman, 1884-1935, Together with Commentary and Notes* (Mellen Press, 2014), a thirty-year project that was awarded the Adele Mellen Prize "for its distinguished contribution to scholarship."

Always a lover of the written word, Markham earned a master's and a doctorate in English and Creative Writing from Florida State University following a bachelors in English from University of Alabama in Huntsville. A recipient of numerous grants and awards for literary merit, including three Georgia Council for the Arts grants, a South Carolina Arts Commission Community Grant, and an Arts Kentucky Women's Foundation Award, she has also served as a humanities scholar. Markham has presented hundreds of papers, lectures, and readings of her original and critical work.

Dr. Markham enjoyed a rich academic career from which she retired as a full professor. She now mentors poets and writers, living and writing near the coast of South Carolina.